Judi Keshet-Orr
Sarah Collings

In the Footsteps of the Fathers

Psychosexual therapy with the Orthodox Jewish community – an overview from the therapist's chair

Hadassa Word Press

Imprint

Any brand names and product names mentioned in this book are subject to trademark, brand or patent protection and are trademarks or registered trademarks of their respective holders. The use of brand names, product names, common names, trade names, product descriptions etc. even without a particular marking in this work is in no way to be construed to mean that such names may be regarded as unrestricted in respect of trademark and brand protection legislation and could thus be used by anyone.

Cover image: www.ingimage.com

Publisher:
Hadassa Word Press
is a trademark of
International Book Market Service Ltd., member of OmniScriptum Publishing Group
17 Meldrum Street, Beau Bassin 71504, Mauritius

Printed at: see last page
ISBN: 978-620-2-45537-4

In the Footsteps of the Fathers:
Psychosexual therapy with the Orthodox Jewish community
– an overview from the therapist's chair

Judi Keshet-Orr & Sarah Collings
Forewords by Rabbi Joel & Ruthie Portnoy
and Margaret Ramage

'The desire to reach for the stars is ambitious. The desire to reach hearts is wise'
Maya Angelou

This text – based on the research and the clinical practice of Judi Keshet-Orr – offers an overview of psychosexual work among the Orthodox Jewish community in the U.K., juxtaposing attitudes to sexual practice in both non-Orthodox Jewish and non-Jewish populations.

It will examine aspects of belief, behaviour and attitude within the Orthodox population and explore how Orthodox teachings on sex might be helpful or unhelpful, both for Orthodox and non-Orthodox people.

It will also explore how therapeutic approaches adopted with the Orthodox Jewish community might benefit psychosexual work with non-Orthodox couples.

Judi Keshet-Orr
Consultant Psychosexual Psychotherapist
Email: judi.weresolve@gmail.com
Web sites:
www.psychosexualtraining.org.uk
www.jkopsychotherapy.co.uk
www.relationshipresolvelondon.org.uk

Sarah Collings
Psychosexual and Relationship Psychotherapist
Email: psyc1sar@aol.com

Contents

Section 1. IN THE FOOTPRINTS OF THE FATHERS:
Psychosexual Therapy and the Orthodox Jewish Community

Section 2. IN THE SHADOW OF ABRAHAM:
Abraham's Legacy

About the Authors

Judi Keshet-Orr MSc UKCP. FCOSRT. FNCP.

Following a career in social work and as a joint investigation training officer, (police and social services) working for statutory and non-statutory agencies, Judi then trained as a psychosexual and relationship psychotherapist at St. George's Hospital, London, post her psychotherapy and group psychotherapy training in London. She has also trained in Family Mediation. Judi holds UKCP/CSRP accredited status

Judi is increasingly involved in training and facilitation of psychotherapists who wish to specialise in the field of psychosexual and relationship therapy. Her particular areas of interest are transgenerational issues, conflict resolution, survivors of abuse and relationship enhancement.

Judi was the first person in the UK to be awarded an MSc in Psychosexual and Relationship Therapy. She is also one of the few people in the UK to hold the European CERTIFICATE in Psychotherapy. Judi was awarded Fellowship status with COSRT (College of Sexual & Relationship Therapy) and the National Counselling Society (NCS) in 2014 for 'outstanding contributions' to the profession.

Judi has founded and co-founded several successful organisations and training programmes. She has contributed to several academic journals, published a number of articles, spoken on radio and appeared on television both in the UK and overseas. She is a regular conference speaker and work shop facilitator in the UK and abroad whilst also maintaining links with a major international organisational development consultancy working in developing countries. She maintains a private practice in London.

Sarah Collings MA MPhil

Sarah was formerly an AHPP (Association of Humanistic Psychology Practitioners) accredited humanistic-integrative psychotherapist, and COSRT accredited psychosexual psychotherapist, and UKCP registered since 2000. With over twenty five years in the field she worked as a psychosexual psychotherapist and supervisor in private practice, primary and secondary care and in the Third Sector since 1995. She has been on the executive committee of CSRP for 5 years and Chaired the then Membership and Accreditation committee at AHPP from 2012-2016. Diagnosed in 2015 with Multiple System Atrophy a progressive degenerative neurological illness, Sarah has therefore had to retire from clinical practice, but still has a deep interest in contributing to the professional field especially around her longstanding interests in sexuality, disability and diversity. This has included working not only with a wide range of ethnicity and faiths as clients, but also colleagues from a plethora of backgrounds and religions/faiths.

Sarah's original training was in Existential psychotherapy. Existential givens have always been the philosophical bedrock of her life and therefore of her work, and seem increasingly relevant under the challenges of her present circumstances. She has also found existential concepts highly relevant when working with any type of diversity and/or psychosexual issue.

Foreword

By Rabbi Joel and Ruthie Portnoy

At last a long overdue book, written by masters in the field of Sex Therapy which tackles a very difficult and growing concern in the Orthodox Jewish World. Written with respect and sensitivity for the Orthodox/Charedi position, as well as that of other major religions, but also setting the scene for what we know as therapists is a very real challenge in 2019.

Having had the privilege of learning in person from Judi Keshet-Orr, we are confident that this work is much more than a piece of academic research. Rather it is a work that takes into account a lifetime of working within the ultra-orthodox Jewish Community where the authors have built up trust and respect despite being regarded as 'outsiders' by a very closed and private community.

The book does not profess to have any answers rather, it challenges the reader/therapist to find out more and to be aware of the background of ultra-orthodox clients. It equips the therapist with a valuable toolbox which will enhance their work and certainly help build up rapport with the Orthodox client. As every therapist knows, building rapport is more than fifty percent of our work.

We hope that this work will become a textbook to which every Psychosexual Therapist will have easy access.

We look forward to the day when appropriate and sensitive sex education, (including educating couples to communicate), will replace the need for so much of the work that we are doing today.

Rabbi Joel and Ruthie Portnoy
Email: 2halvesofasoul.com
Manchester U.K.

Foreword

By Margaret Ramage

I am delighted to write the foreword for this rather unusual book. My interest in it and enthusiasm for it come from my experience of practising as a psychosexual therapist, supervisor and teacher across many religions and cultures within the UK. It fills a gap in the usual psychosexual literature, is written in an intimate, non-technical style and will be of interest across many professional disciplines.

Here we are presented with two contrasting chapters by authors who are each experts in this field. They write from related but different viewpoints, and in some areas, they cover the same ground, each from their own personal therapeutic and academic perspectives. Any therapist would find this material enlightening and useful. Both authors impart their knowledge with ease and fluency, being accustomed to addressing a range of audiences from the psychotherapeutic and other disciplines.

Judi Keshet-Orr is a renowned teacher and trainer of Psychosexual Therapy and has probably trained more psychosexual therapists from the UK and worldwide than anybody else in Britain. She first published on the topic of Jewish Women and Sexuality in 2003, and in her chapter here she refers to the research she undertook for that paper, as well as drawing on the multiplicity of her subsequent therapeutic contacts with couples from the Jewish Communities. Another resource for her has been from the training courses she created for Jewish therapists and for other communities. She has deep knowledge and understanding of Judaism today, and she offers a broad therapeutic tapestry, touching on the range in modalities of psychotherapy, the importance of the therapeutic relationship, and in particular the types of problems facing Jewish and other couples in the modern world.

Sarah Collings is a highly respected humanistic psychotherapist and psychosexual therapist, who has specialist training in cross cultural therapy. She has given her expertise to national therapeutic organisational efforts related to standards of practice, and has written about many aspects of sexuality and psychosexual therapy from both academic and clinical perspectives. Her chapter gives the reader a historical overview of the founding of the three main monotheistic religions, and the laws, attitudes and prohibitions that they foster towards sexuality. She also offers some tips for therapists to help them in their own reflections, and how to avoid some of the likely pitfalls that may exist when working with any couple, whatever their culture or religion.

Both authors naturally refer to the devastating impact of the Holocaust on Judaism today. Therapists learned of the phenomenon of intergenerational transmission of trauma from their clinical experiences, and recent advances in neuroscience have served to confirm the reverberating effects of national trauma such as war and the Holocaust, as well as familial abuse, again referred to here from each author in her own terms.

This is a book for all therapists, it is compact, which is an advantage given the vast quantity of written material confronting us, and covers much that is valuable for professionals of any discipline who work amongst communities from cultures and religions different from their own. I found it a fascinating read and it is my hope that it reaches the wide circulation it deserves.

Margaret Ramage
Fellow COSRT. UKCP Honorary Fellowship
London U.K.

Acknowledgments

I would like to thank, in the first instance, my clients and trainees who have shown me many of the puzzles and mysteries which they have faced and have allowed me the privilege of knowing and working with them. My trusted and loved colleagues, who have supported and followed my work for over thirty years and particularly Sarah Collings who has contributed to this book and whose intelligence, wisdom and kindness has known no bounds. Finally, my family and friends who remain my greatest advocates.

Judi Keshet-Orr

Firstly, I would like to thank all my clients who put the flesh on theory and brought the whole process of therapy to life; you taught me so much. As did the many colleagues over the years, some of whom I feel very honoured to count as friends now, in particular Judi Keshet-Orr who has been a deeply kind and loyal friend and mentor, and to whom I am forever indebted for her wisdom and support. And much loving gratitude to my Oxford family for their unswerving belief that water is there to be walked on.

Sarah Collings

1

IN THE FOOTPRINTS OF THE FATHERS

Psychosexual Therapy and
the Orthodox Jewish Community

Introduction

"Nothing makes religious people as nervous as sex, or at least unregulated sex." –Berne (1973, p. 23)

This chapter will focus on what benefits may be derived from 'kosher sex', a term popularised in an influential book authored by Shmuley Boteach (1999). In particular, I will focus on the traditional Orthodox Jewish community, which is itself divided into several sub-groups (Orthodox Jewry is not an integrated organisation with a single administrative body, but several alternative movements abiding by common principles).

These musings, from the therapist's chair, are resultant from my subjective experience of working with both Orthodox and non-Orthodox communities. I hope this work will encourage creativity in the field of psychosexual work with this community, perhaps by helping therapists to feel less daunted, in keeping with the approach of Jewish Action and Training for Sexual Health:

> "If sex is mysterious, anxious, angry, threatening or guilt provoking, we run the risk of alienating those we wish to protect."

To begin, I think it is possible to spell out briefly the parameters of psychosexual and relationship therapy from the perspective of integrative therapy, which is the modality I work in. We can say that the aim of therapy is to enable and encourage clients to have an enhanced experience of love, intimacy, sensuality, relationality, communication and sexuality. However, at the outset of therapy, therapists will typically encounter clients who express shame, confusion, naivety, guilt, disappointment, secrecy, anger and rage. There are many means that can be adopted by the therapist, and, indeed, I believe the ability to be flexible in the work, which is an integral aspect of integrative therapy, is crucial – as will be seen. For my own work, I draw in particular on Humanistic, Cognitive Behavioural Therapy, psychodynamic theory and medical perspectives. In particular, I place an emphasis on exploring the familial history that has informed the relationship style of the couple or individual. The aim is to help individuals and couples to acquire a sense of personal empowerment and a sense of equality in their relationships.

In integrative therapy, we tend to work relationally. Rather than speaking about 'cure', we focus on collaborative work in which the therapeutic alliance itself becomes a model for relating that can be internalised by the client. Working relationally means that the therapist is 'in the room', which means there will be times when the therapist will introduce alternative viewpoints that might challenge clients by offering fresh perspectives which they can draw on and employ if they wish. This aspect of therapy is particularly pertinent in that therapists working in the Orthodox community might find themselves challenging the belief systems of clients. For this reason, in working relationally, it is essential that the therapist has worked through their own attitudes to sexual attitudes and religious teachings, and that they are sensitive regarding the impact that their beliefs about gender, ethnicity, faith and culture might have as part of the complex therapeutic alliance.

In the current era, we can see how many communities are benefiting from a growing awareness in matters of sexuality, sexual function, and relational communication. However, despite these advances, those from minority religious, ethnic or cultural groups – which typically have strict rulings around sexual practice – have largely been overlooked within the literature and within dedicated psychosexual training environments. This text will therefore attempt to address this deficit, with a specific focus on the Orthodox Jewish community. That said, I trust that some of my observations regarding this community may prove applicable as general principles for working with other groups.

Attitudes to sex in the Orthodox community

"Religion and justice may stand in contradiction, but the humane must always triumph." (p.34 S. Heschel -Gender in Judaism & Islam)

Generally, within the Orthodox community, courtships are brief. Introductions are typically made through family friends and networking. Marriage partners are often young – typically male and female, both aged below 25, heterosexuality is assumed. Decisions to marry are frequently made within weeks or just a few months. There will have been no sex or intimate contact before the wedding night, and little in terms of sex education. At the same time, there is a hope and an expectation that the new couple will bond quickly and produce many children.

This situation has prompted a number of writers to call for more sex education in Orthodox communities. Lasson (2000) has called for more dialogue during the marriage preparation stage between the Shadchan (traditional matchmaker) and Kallah (bride instructor). However, these figures are often in need of further psychosexual education themselves, as Rosenbaum (2015) has observed:

> "...as a number of kallah instructors have admitted, some kallah teachers are un-intentionally sending incorrect, and possibly damaging messages. The impact of negative sexual messages or

misguided information, can last several years into marriage, as I have learned from my clinical practice as a couples and sex therapist."

Also arguing for improved education, Maybruch, Pirutinsky and Pelcovitz (2014) studied religious premarital education among 1,244 married Orthodox Jews and concluded:

"Education focusing on the religious approach and practices regarding the sexual relationship is significantly associated with greater marital quality. [Our] findings also suggest a need for increased premarital education related to communication and conflict resolution."

An Orthodox Jewish wedding is accompanied by a distinct set of rituals, including the public endorsement of a contract between the bride and groom, called a *ketubah*, which is an ancient text written primarily in Talmudic-Aramaic. An Orthodox wedding ceremony may last no longer than an hour, but subsequent celebrations may include a series of meals over a period of a week during which the bride and groom are blessed with seven blessings or, in Hebrew, *sheva brachot.*

Non-Orthodox couples will typically compose parts of the marriage contract themselves, meaning the contract will be less traditional in its imperatives. And, in the case of some same sex couples and those who are less observant, a *ketubah* will still be produced but the text is likely to be highly personalised.

Whilst for some couples, marriage is the first step to love, as they may understand it, for others it is not. Sexual naivety, fear or recognition that an inappropriate choice has been made can lead to a life of pain, hardship and discordance. Indeed, there are many couples who present in therapy during the first year of married life, and the underlying issue can broadly be recognised as painful disappointment. There are manifestations of psychosexual issues that are largely due to a lack of information and education, the most common are generally non-consummation, dyspareunia, vaginismus, rapid ejaculation and erectile failure.

Orthodox law

Any attempt to offer psychosexual therapy to the Orthodox Jewish community must take into account Jewish law. In accordance with this law, Orthodox Jews adopt a sexual contact that is based on teachings from the Old Testament, as explained and expanded upon by classical rabbinic teaching.

Jewish law is derived from two sources. The first is the Scriptures, known as the Torah, which is the Five Books of Moses, this is referred to as Written Law. The second source is the Talmud and Codes, which is referred to as Oral Law. The Talmud is comprised largely of a second-century rabbinic document known as the Mishna, together with the Gemara, which is a commentary on the Mishna. As there are many contradictions and tensions within these teachings, rabbinical discourse has been an important ongoing part of Jewish life and tradition since the creation of these various documents.

Conventionally, the marriage contract states that outside of pregnancy or when nursing the newborn, in each month there should be two weeks given to physical love/contact, and two weeks in which the couple abstain and focus instead on intellectual pursuits, conversation and emotional bonding. The intention is that sexual contact will occur while the woman is ovulating and at her most fertile, while the two weeks of sexual abstinence coincide with menstruation, when the woman is considered ritually impure. The two weeks of abstinence concludes with a week in which menstrual flow ceases and the woman attends a ritual bath, called a *mikveh*, where she immerses herself in a pool of water as an act of purification. This cycle becomes quickly established for the new couple.

The upside of this arrangement is that it can facilitate sexual desire, which can grow in anticipation of the woman becoming available for sex. By contrast, another possible advantage of this routine is that in discordant, loveless or problematic marriages this strict routine affords the parties 'time out' from any sexual obligations. It is interesting to consider how this routine-led approach might be translated into work with non-Jewish couples and to consider the periods of sexual abstinence as having a positive impact on the couple relationship. However, attention would need to be paid to Orthodox women who have irregular menstrual cycles especially if their periods are frequent, thus causing confusion regarding the woman's state of ritual purity.

Sex therapy

Given the difficulties in broaching sexual and profoundly intimate matters in orthodox Jewish communities, it is ironic that, historically, psychotherapy was once commonly referred to as 'the Jewish science'. Indeed, much of the theory that modern integrative psychosexual therapists draw upon was first proposed by Jewish therapists, including Wilhelm Reich, Fritz Perls, Jack Rosenberg and Abraham Maslow.

During the formative years of psychosexual therapy, the emphasis was on short-term behavioural techniques. Subsequently, a more relational approach was adopted by the early integrative therapists, who all espoused a life-affirming view of sexuality: a belief that people have the right to develop, pursue and enjoy the innate, and often powerful, sexual drive.

Today, psychosexual theory is enhanced by a capacity to draw upon an increasingly wide theory base, including behaviourism, medicine, psychotherapy and numerous technique-based treatments, including training in motivational techniques, relationship enhancement (IMAGO) and communication skills.

However, most training in psychosexual therapy, in the UK especially, continues to be centered around the work of Masters and Johnson (Weiner & Avery-Clark, 2017), who proposed the 'sensate focus' programme. However, this system, which adopts a psychologically behavioural approach, fails to address, with any depth the emotional, spiritual, social, ethnic and cultural reality of clients. Furthermore, the programme does not address the cultural mores of most minority groups, including Orthodox Jews. For example, a traditional sensate focus programme encourages couples to have intimate contact on an almost daily basis, which therefore puts it outside the realms of Orthodox teachings and rules. Happily, though, attempts have been made to adapt the programme for the Orthodox community. In particular, Ribner and Rosenfeld (McDonough, 2003) broke new ground in highlighting the need for psychosexual education in the Orthodox community. Here is an extract from a BBC article based on an interview with the two authors:

"Sex is only appropriate within a marital context," [Ribner] says. "Beyond that it's not talked about. Because of that, it's become very difficult for people to have any kind of dialogue about it."

Orthodox couples often see pre-marital counselling before their wedding to learn about sex and about Jewish religious laws of menstrual purity. But on their wedding night, many newly-weds still find themselves unprepared.

"It's embarrassing to have to call a [pre-marital] teacher in the middle of the night... but many people do,' says the book's co-author Jennie Rosenfeld. 'Others suffer in silence and try to muddle through."

In Israel's Orthodox and ultra-Orthodox community, there are manuals written for brides and grooms to be, to help guide them on the subject of intimacy in married life, but they employ allegorical, vague terminology and no explicit how-to instructions on matters of sexual intercourse.

Other authors who have made valuable contributions that support sex therapy with the Jewish community include Boyarin, Klienplatz and Rosenbaum.

In my own work, I hold the view that it is the relationship itself between therapist and client that has the power to generate healing and increased awareness. For me, the crucible of the relationship is a robust frame in which the therapist can negotiate and work with contradictions in belief systems. In this regard, the therapist can help to create a space in which clients feel safe enough to challenge their beliefs and consider different viewpoints. This will allow for a dialogue that respects the beliefs of the client while also giving the client an opportunity to experience and negotiate difference of opinion. It is at this relational edge that I believe the therapist can work most usefully through modelling relationship in the room.

Working in the Jewish community

Broadly speaking, Jews are divided into two ethnic groups. Sephardic Jews are generally accepted as those who originate from Spain, Portugal, Iran, Iraq, North Africa and India. Ashkenazi Jews are those who originate from Germany, and can be Polish, Galician, Romanian, Russian, Lithuanian, Dutch, Austrian and Hungarian, and are of Eastern European decent. A lesser used term is that of Mizrahim that specifically denotes those who originate from Asia and North Africa.

In addition to these ethnic divisions, there are also divisions based on interpretations of the law, including Masorti, Conservative, Liberal, Reform and Orthodox Jews, who differ with regard to their adherence to traditional tenets and convictions. The more progressive affiliations, such as Reform or Liberal Judaism, reject the entire concept of religious regulations for sex and gender issues, for example they will ordain women rabbis, which is wholly unacceptable in the Orthodox tradition. Masorti and Conservative Jews espouse a more ambivalent attitude and tend to be selective in their approach. Orthodox Jews are notionally totally committed to strict observance of the laws, but there are variations with regard to interpretation due to differences of opinion between rabbis, for example with regard to contraceptive techniques and other modern innovations, which would include assisted conception and the use of PDE5s (Viagra, Cialis, Vardenafil, etc.).

Many Orthodox Jews tend to obey a distinctive dress code, although this may vary depending on the level of observance and which group the person is affiliated with. For women, dress is typically modest, with little or no skin displayed apart from the face, neck, lower arms and hands; married women cover their heads and often wear a wig or some form of head covering; men will mostly wear dark suits, white shirts and *kippot*, and they wear a vest with fringes called *tzitzit*, hanging from their clothes. Commenting on gender differences in the Orthodox community, Boteach (1999, p. 225) states:

> "Rules insist that men and women dress differently, pray separated by a divider called a mechitzah, and that women never be thrust too far into positions of great exposure that might rob them of their natural mystery."

However, it must be kept in mind that the Orthodox Jewish community is not a single group, but consists of people from different backgrounds and cultures, with different interpretations of Jewish law. Perhaps the most notable sub-division within the Orthodox tradition is the distinction between the ultra-Orthodox or Haredi groups (including so-called Hasidic Jews) and what is termed modern-Orthodox. To the ultra-Orthodox, the modern-Orthodox community is seen as cutting corners with respect to their adherence to the law. It can be seen, therefore, that there are many complexities and intricacies between the various groups in Jewry.

It is no surprise then that in my work as a psychosexual and relationship therapist in Jewish communities I frequently encounter clients with strong religious affiliations and beliefs. As seen earlier, much of the theory for psychosexual therapy is at variance with these affiliations and beliefs. It therefore requires considerable creativity on the part of the therapist to find a meaningful approach that can be useful for such clients. Even so, it is almost inevitable that therapy will challenge clients' belief systems and values around sex and gender norms. Therapists – in particular those working with the Orthodox community – could therefore expect a high degree of resistance, reticence or shyness in the consulting rooms. There are also interesting implications here for the supervision process, in which we can expect highly charged counter-transferential re-enactments – and so there is perhaps a case here for Jewish therapists to seek out supervision with both Jewish and non-Jewish supervisors.

Complexities in working with the Orthodox community

Given the complexity of Jewish cultural variations, it potentially could be rare or unusual that the cultural beliefs of the therapist exactly match those of the client (if, indeed, this was possible or desirable).

However, there is strong support for therapists who wish to work across cultural and ethnic divides, in particular this can be found in the work of Weiner (1991) who developed the concept of ethnotherapy, about which he explains:

> Ethnotherapy seeks to move people from conflicts in their identity to a more secure and positive grounding in their group, as well as more positive self-esteem. Personal problems are then seen through an ethnic lens in their defining social context.

Being able to see through an 'ethnic lens' is therefore a key skill, which could be seen as a more sophisticated form of empathy, a significant tool for any type of therapist.

In the process, as mentioned above, Jewish psychosexual and relationship therapists working with Jewish clients will find themselves challenged, and will be faced with a need to explore their own feelings and attitudes towards different aspects of Jewishness. Similarly, non-Jewish therapists will need to confront their attitudes to Judaism in all its forms. Of course, such self-awareness in the therapist is relevant when working with anyone with a different culture, ethnicity or value/biosocial system. ·

For many Orthodox Jews, personal beliefs and a perceived difference in values make it unlikely that they will consider psychotherapy of any kind. For those who do want to seek help, a first appropriate step would be to seek the counsel of their rabbi. However, an increasing number of Orthodox Jews are now approaching therapists (Neroulias, 2011). This is something I have observed in my own work. In 2015, in Belgium, I taught a group of Jewish women who later opened their own counselling centre for children and young people; and in 2016 I ran a two-year training course in psychosexual and relationship therapy for therapists from the Orthodox community who, unusually, were a mixed group of men and women – I was invited to do this after they identified a growing need for psychosexual work in their community. A further observation regarding trends is that those in the Orthodox community often seek out therapists who are not Orthodox (such as myself and colleagues), which I believe is because they want to speak to someone from outside their relatively-small community due to anxieties around possibly breaches in confidentiality.

Orthodox teachings on sex

In working with the Orthodox Jewish community, we must be mindful of the traditional perception which states that rigid boundaries are necessary and essential to preserve Jewishness. This is how Plaskow (1991, p. 179) explains the Orthodox standpoint:

The heart of Jewish ambivalence toward sexuality is roughly this: the sexual impulse is given by God and thus is a normal and healthy part of Jewish life. Sexual relations are appropriate only within the framework of heterosexual marriage, but within marriage, they are good, indeed, commanded. Yet sexuality even within marriage also requires careful, sometimes rigorous control, in order that it not transgress the boundaries of marriage or the laws of niddah [a menstruating woman] within it.

The Orthodox community is heteronormative in its attitudes to sex, with same sex or multiple relationships seen only in critical or negative terms in Jewish law. The emphasis is on marriage and procreation. The husband should endeavour to produce at least two children, one of each sex. Where children cannot be conceived, a divorce can be granted, by either the husband or wife. For the wife, not having children attacks the foundation of her gender role. However, for many, these are becoming increasingly outdated views, with more aware/modern Orthodox people now holding different views. This is evidenced, for example, by the fact there is now in London a service for assisted conception for Jewish couples (www.chana.org.uk).

A common belief, which is often echoed in the therapy room, states that sexual intercourse should be conducted in the missionary position, with the lights off, at predetermined times according to the menstrual cycle. However, in practice, Orthodox clients are often considerably more creative. Indeed, within Judaism as a whole there are endless discourses around what is and is not permissible. Rabbis are consulted, books are written and re-written, and the most religious and observant are questioned. With this in mind, I believe it is valid to suggest to clients that there is no 'one truth' in Judaism, but rather a long tradition of debate that dates back centuries. Indeed, Rambam (Mishne Torah, Hilkhot Issurei Biah 21:10), a medieval Jewish philosopher, has stated:

"A man may do whatever he wants with his wife. He may have intercourse with her at any time, and may kiss her on whatever limb of her body he wants. He may even engage in unnatural sex."

In the modern era, Orthodoxy has been challenged by popular Jewish novelists, such as Jong, Miller, Roth and Potok, who have attempted to show how Jewish practice is a conglomeration of mythology and caricature, but, rather than discrediting this state of affairs entirely, they allow that there are aspects of truth to be found in stereotypes and tradition (a case of not throwing out the baby with the bathwater). Of particular interest is that these authors' part-autobiographical novels challenge gender stereotypes, such as Jong's varying portrayals of women, from rapacious sexual beings to archetypal matriarchs.

In similar vein, Weeks argues for ongoing debate on sexual matters, rather than adherence to a strict system of laws; he writes (1987, p. 31):

"Sexual identity and sexual desire are not fixed and unchanging. We create boundaries and identities for ourselves to contain what might otherwise threaten to engulf or dissolve into formlessness."

We can see that the debate around sexuality in Jewish culture runs deep – and the stakes are high. Indeed, for many Jewish women, the observance of traditional mores and values is essential for ensuring the continuing identity of the Jewish people. Indeed, Judaism has rarely regarded celibacy as having religious or spiritual worth. Regarding sexual activity itself, there remains latitude in traditional writings for what is permissible to facilitate pleasure. It is therefore confusing that many Jews who wish to uphold the law will also deny themselves permission to experiment in order to seek more intense experiences. In my opinion, this is a further indication that there is a need for better psychoeducation among Orthodox people, a view which is supported by Rosenbaum (cited in Katsman, 2008), who highlights the pressing need to help young Orthodox couples:

Patience and kindness is nice, but if sexual education is not provided by madrichim and madrichot (counselling who teach brides and grooms Jewish law relevant to marriage), couples will look for it through other resources, including the internet and books. Some of what they find may be OK, but much of it may be misinformation, or not culturally sensitive to Orthodox people...

In the Orthodox community sexuality is not generally viewed as a developmental process, but rather as something that becomes relevant once you are married. This is challenging for many reasons. One is that young people are often at a loss regarding how to deal with their sexual feelings, may be used to repressing them, or feeling guilty about them, and then suddenly need to view those feelings and experience them differently. Another, is that the expectation to go from complete sexual inexperience to complete intercourse in one or two nights is a difficult one.

Finally, the transitions in the beginning from no touching at all to being sexual are often very difficult for a newly married couple... especially after that first time when they have to separate.

Clearly sex information and education play an important part in determining later sexual attitudes and practices. However, within formal Jewish education, there appears to be little or no formal and accurate sex education. We may also question how good or accurate sex education and relationship skills information is within the wider public.

In my own experience of working with the Orthodox community, I have at times been alarmed by the lack of understanding and an absence of vocabulary regarding sexual topics. In the Orthodox community, an enormous amount of misinformation is being circulated, often via folklore or myth, with a corresponding lack of alternative perspectives due to prohibitions on books and films containing sexual material. As a consequence, much of my psychosexual work has and continues to involve a measure of sex education – which requires a high level of creativity when working with observant Orthodox clients. For example, while traditional teaching means the clients are unlikely to want to look at photographs or film, the therapist can seek the permission of clients to make drawings of genitalia and sex acts.

A study with Jewish women

In 1995 I undertook research on Jewish women living in London, aged between 23 and 67 years (n=36). I asked about their experiences in psychotherapy and psychosexual therapy, specifically its impact on their lives in the context of being Jewish. All the women said therapy had given them a language to understand and express their sexuality in ways that had previously been denied. At a simple level, the therapeutic alliance had given these women accurate and factual information about anatomy and physiology and a safe environment in which to explore their concerns.

The women I interviewed had diverse experiences of psychosexual therapy, both medium- and long-term, with behavioural, psychodynamic and humanistic therapists. I was therefore able to deduce that it was the therapists themselves, and not their particular school or method, that had facilitated change, which I surmised they achieved by creating a dialogic environment in which the women could feel validated and encouraged to explore sexual, sensual and intimacy concerns. For example, therapy had enabled these women to confront issues such as monogamy, sexual orientation, and divorce. An important factor was that the women were able to undertake an in-depth exploration of the meaning of their Jewishness in relation to their sexuality.

Here are some of the comments I gathered as part of the research:

"Being Jewish is me, therefore it must affect my sexuality."

> "Being Jewish is a fundamental part of my identity, it informs me physically and emotionally."

> "Being Jewish informs my sexuality, I idealise family values."

> "I feel bad and guilty for not wanting or taking pleasure in sex at the 'right' times."

> "How do I, as a Jewish woman, teach my sons and daughters about sex and how do I teach them to have views which are open and consistent with Judaism?"

Clearly, a sense of Jewishness could not be disassociated from these women's experience of sexuality.

My research invited these women to explore the impact of Jewish law on their sexuality. Broadly speaking, the women fell into two distinct categories. One group on the whole upheld all the rules and traditions. The other group indicated a greater awareness of the importance of feminist politics and opted out of much of the tradition – choosing not to observe many rituals, holidays and high holy days – while maintaining a hold on what they perceived to be their essential Jewishness and birth right, which they described varyingly as a felt sense, an association, and the feeling of being part of a minority group and community; this group did not completely dismiss tradition, but they chose to find their own way through the various contradictions between tradition and feminism. Heschel describes the outlook of Jewish women who struggle with tradition. She writes (1990, p. 39):

> For Jewish women who do not see themselves reflected in the images and roles set forth by classical Judaism, the task is to develop an identity that will combine the values of feminism with those of Judaism. Feminist therapists can be crucial in making women

aware that the negative stereotypes regarding femaleness they have internalised are derived from classical male authored Jewish texts.

All of the women I spoke to in my study said they had discussed these matters in personal therapy. One of the consequences was that family and community norms were being confronted and re-evaluated – which could be both liberating and challenging for clients as they started to question what it meant to be Jewish and what this might mean for the preservation of the faith. For the integrative therapist, the challenge is to be aware of any self-bias and how this might impact on the therapy. For example, to what extent will the therapist be able to hold a neutral stance when it seems desirable that a client should deny aspects of Jewish law in favour of an acceptance of a stance that is more affirming of the rights of women? When working within the Orthodox community these issues become even more heightened and sharply focused.

One issue which I have encountered numerous times is that many Jewish men have been raised to believe that unless they are in control sexually then the experience of sex is a negative or humiliating one. In this context, it can be seen how the sexually liberated woman might pose a threat. One way that men deal with this is to demonise women (Judaism is no exception in this). One particular powerful archetypal image that I have been able to explore in therapy with those from the Jewish community is the story of Lilith, the folkloric companion of Adam who predated Eve. Lilith is a long-haired temptress who represents a powerful female sexuality; she also has murderous tendencies. She has been embraced by many feminists as an archetypal figure who represents independence and autonomy for women (Gaines, 2018). As such, she challenges tradition, which would include much of Orthodox culture – and no doubt this is the reason why the Lilith figure has been demonised. Indeed, in the Orthodox community, there is a myth, taken seriously by many, that Lilith has dominion over the life and death of children until they are eight days old (Hammer, 2018). There is therefore an implication, as expressed in the demonisation of Lilith, that disregarding tradition, for example by allowing challenging gender stereotypes and allowing more independence for women, is to put at serious risk the future of the Jewish race.

Sexuality in light of the Holocaust

The preservation of the Jewish race is a part of Jewish sexuality. Indeed, my own research highlighted for me how the personal, communal and cultural are entwined. Many clients will be just one or two generations removed from the horror of the Holocaust, which raises questions around transgenerational trauma. What, therefore, are the ramifications of the Holocaust on Jews today – their ongoing sense of place and safety – and how might we encounter this in the therapy room? In Britain today many Jews are again fearful and considering migration to what they perceive is a safer place.

Until the creation of the State of Israel, Jews in modern times did not have a 'homeland'. Instead, Jews had to deal with questions of assimilation – considering the extent to which they were willing or able to fit in with the surrounding culture, which would include a consideration of non-Jewish attitudes to gender and sexuality. For the different Jewish groups, was assimilation permissible or otherwise? To what extent is the consideration and integration of 'non-Jewish' ideas acceptable – and how do such questions play out in the Jewish community and in the therapy room? Psychically speaking, the creation of Israel added a new dimension to this debate given that, for many, there is now a place of safety or sanctuary, which arguably lessens any compulsion to assimilate to non-Jewish values. The precise nature of Jewish values is an ongoing debate – and the Orthodox community, in its variations, will hold particular views on this.

It is incumbent on Jews to have a view on these matters, although some, whether through choice or denial, will avoid the question. For some, especially those in the Orthodox community, the solution is to keep themselves to themselves as much as possible by living in Orthodox communities that are as self-sufficient as possible – and, indeed, there are many lively and vibrant Orthodox communities worldwide who have set up what could be regarded as modern time shtetel (small Jewish towns or villages). Such communities are typically viewed with curiosity, fear or prejudice by non-Jews and some less observant Jews, and often they become a target for anti-Semitism and the misguided attitudes and beliefs of those around them.

All of these issues are a part of the picture in therapy with Jews, including psychosexual therapy, and it is not going away. To explain further, there is little doubt that Holocaust survivors and refugees have passed on various beliefs and values to their children and grandchildren, creating much confusion, anxiety and pain. One commonly understood notion is the idea that the 1.5 million children who died in the concentration camps need to be replaced so that families might be rebuilt. This sentiment was expressed by a Jewish psychotherapist, as reported by Baker (1993, p. 158):

> You know, I've got no family; my mother came to this country as a child and all her family perished; my father's parents died, too, when he was little and he was separated from his only sister. The most important thing for me to do was to become a mother, a Jewish mother.

For my own experience as a therapist and personal observation, I have little doubt that the imperative for marriage and procreation is a fundamental part of being Jewish in that they are vitally connected to anxieties regarding the continuation and preservation of the Jewish people. Some of the implications for psychosexual therapy are clear. Couples within the Orthodox community, for example, often have many children, frequently running in to double figures; aside from a few exceptional circumstances, the use of birth control is frowned upon when there is no contra-indication regarding the mental or physical health of child or mother. This might include a woman, after having four children, inclusive of both a boy and a girl being given 'permission' to use birth control if it were perceived that any more would be a real struggle and potentially detrimental to her health. Children are always seen as a blessing within the family.

Another aspect of the Holocaust that we must consider is the brutalisation of the racial psyche. One response is a deeply ingrained determination that Jews must ensure that they are never again so vulnerable, but must remain resolute in seeking the continuation of the line. Clearly, this will have a profound impact on attitudes regarding children and family values, and this will be encountered in the therapy room.

In traditional and Orthodox Judaism, the Jewish line is continued through the mother, even where the father is a non-Jew. Jews do not seek converts; however, some of the Orthodox and, in my experience, non-orthodox community do not fully accept those who do convert to Judaism. (Whilst not seeking converts there is a movement of those called *baal teshuvah* which denotes secular Jews returning to a more religious and observant form of Judaism). Hence, there is a concern in many communities, and a pressure on women, for Jewish women to put their sexuality and fertility at the service of the community. In this sense, the Jewish woman's sexuality is not entirely her own – which, again, flags up the sorts of dilemmas that Jewish people might bring to psychosexual therapy.

Judaism and its teachings regarding women are peppered with contradictions: while women are seen as sexual beings with rights and needs of their own, they are also required to fulfil their husband's needs, sexually and as a child-bearer and home-maker. And there is a strong compulsion to uphold this cultural arrangement, with enormous pressure put on the husband and wife to remain faithful. Indeed, having children is so important that early marriages are encouraged, especially in the Orthodox community. Hence, the cultural norm for exclusive relationships is central to Judaism (although, in reality, we know that this is not always the case).

Remaining single is strongly discouraged. Single Jewish men are viewed with some suspicion and encouraged, even obliged, to marry early. There is strong halachic encouragement for widowers and divorced men to find a spouse as soon as possible rather than remain alone. For women, Jewish law allows that a woman may remain unmarried and childless, but in practice a woman who chooses a single life would be frowned upon, and rabbinical interpretation states that she would be 'unfulfilled'; the Talmud sees companionship as a paramount to a woman. Hence, the pressure to marry is difficult to resist, particularly within the Orthodox community.

While heterosexual marriage is championed, Jewish law simultaneously lists many other sorts of relationship that are not permitted; these include incestuous relationships, mixed or trans-religious relationships, adulterous relationships, relationship with anyone born from a forbidden relationship, and same sex relationships. Such views are in line with all conservative forms of religion.

However, it must be remembered that within the more liberal forms of practicing Judaism, as with Reform and Liberal same sex relationships are sanctioned. Female Rabbis are ordained. Reform Judaism stated, in 2015:

> In 2015, the Reform Jewish Movement led the religious community in affirming the rights of transgender and gender non-conforming people: "Affirms its commitment to the full equality, inclusion, and acceptance of people of all gender identities and gender expressions."

All of the foregoing may come to light in psychosexual therapy – with the weight of cultural fears and expectations hanging heavy on the individual or couple; and all of this must be navigated by the therapist.

Child abuse

In my experience, child sexual abuse is rarely openly discussed within the Jewish community. This also has implications for therapy. In almost every case, a survivor of abuse will not have disclosed the abuse to their spouse, and there will be little or no sense of how abuse can impact on the capacity of an individual to be intimate. Accordingly, a young couple may arrive in therapy with a presenting issue, such as non-consummation, and, in the case of abuse, uncovering the underlying cause will be slow work for the therapist. Consequently, when considered alongside the lack of sex education in many Jewish communities, it can be seen how cases of abuse will prove especially challenging for therapists who must navigate non-disclosure and a lack of understanding; in my practice I have noticed such difficulties are particularly present in work with Orthodox couples.

In my view, there is a vital need to address more fully issues of child sexual abuse among Jewish children. The matter was highlighted by the Independent newspaper (Fenton, 2016), which read:

> Kol v'Oz, a global organisation dedicated to preventing abuse of Jewish children, has formally written to the U.K.'s investigations body for child abuse urging action.

> In a letter to the Independent Inquiry for Child Sexual Abuse (IICSA), Chief Executive Manny Waks wrote: "The IICSA notes that it will investigate a wide range of institutions, including those who fall under the category of 'other religious organisations'. I would like to take this opportunity to encourage the IICSA to seriously consider including at least a segment of the Jewish community in its investigations."

> "In the past few years there have been numerous reports of troubling incidents within the Jewish community; more

specifically, within the Haredi (ultra-Orthodox) community in the UK, including a series of reports by The Independent which note that child sexual abuse is alleged to have occurred in illegal Jewish ultra-Orthodox schools and that authorities turned a blind eye to these schools due, in part, to the fear of being accused of anti-Semitism," Mr. Waks added.

The article quote above addressed specifically the sexual abuse of boys and young men, highlighting the fact that it is not only girls and women who are being sexually abused, nor are all the abuser's men. As stated, abuse is almost always covered up and undisclosed, but it can emerge in couple/relationship therapy and will most likely be something that is having a significant impact on sexual function. Thus, psychosexual therapy must steer a careful passage through past trauma, with the therapist urged to practice caution given that the occasional clumsiness in sexual work might re-stimulate a trauma that one or both partners in a couple might be hiding. Pace and sensitivity are key. With this in mind, the NSPCC (2018) lists that some of the possible consequences of abuse that might present in adulthood, which include:

- Anxiety, depression and self-esteem issues;

- Flashbacks, nightmares and day mares/intrusive thoughts;

- Communication issues;

- Psychosomatic pain;

- Struggles with parenting and intimate relationships;

- Disordered eating;

- Suicidal ideation.

Any of these presentations listed above will impact on how we offer therapy, and the learning curve for the couple will be steep. Given the complexity of these issues, I would therefore advise that psychosexual therapists working with the Jewish community should also have had comprehensive training in general psychotherapy.

It is also important to be mindful of the requirements of UK law, particularly the Sexual Offences Act 2003, which states that religious law is not enforceable by the courts (England and Wales); in fact, the effectiveness of religious law is entirely dependent on an individual's adherence to it. In other words, UK law supersedes any suggestion of religious law when it comes to confidentiality in matters of child or sexual abuse.

Transgender/gender dysphoria

The issue of transgender and gender dysphoria is not widely discussed in Jewish communities. However, as seen, any variations from heteronormative relationships are generally disallowed by Jewish law, particularly in Orthodox communities. Hence, here is a potential population of clients that is not likely to seek out a Jewish, even a religious-orientated, therapist due to the assumptions of clients that their way of life will not be accepted.

However, there are signs that attitudes are changing and becoming more accepting. For example, an article confronting issues pertaining to transgender people appeared in The Times of Israel in 2016, which is perhaps an indication that a debate has started and that opinion is being sought from a variety of learned sources.

Sex in society

Another issue likely to arise in psychosexual work is that of cybersex, porn and sex addition.

Pornography is frowned upon by most Jewish communities, and certainly within Orthodox communities. Pornography, an active interest in sexuality, and even public displays of sexuality all fly in the face of the rules of modesty held by Orthodox people – and this creates inevitable dilemmas as clients try to resolve the competing claims of cultural norms with inner sexual compulsions.

As with most religious communities, there is a debate regarding the degree to which a person can control their sexuality. For example, there is a debate around whether sex addiction is a disease that individuals need help to contain, or whether it is more a question of personal choice and will power. (Of course, religious questions about the strength of self-will and choice reach beyond matters of sexuality).

Within the Jewish community, many sources of teaching are dominated by heteronormative perspectives. Jewish websites, such as Chabad (Guard Your Eyes), are peppered with heterosexual viewpoints, often referring to men as addicts and women as the temptresses who offer porn and cybersex. This explicit heterosexual stance is an indication of how far the debate needs to progress within the community. Indeed, pornography itself is certainly not heteronormative and, as such, the Jewish community needs to confront its outdated and (mostly) unhelpful beliefs, which foster feelings of secrecy and shame (Samoylov, 2018).

Some of these topics fall within the realms of general psychotherapy, but it is also an area of specialism for which psychotherapists will benefit from undertaking specialist training.

Disability

Another client group which needs acknowledgement are those clients with disabilities. Goodwach (2005) states:

People with disabilities learn that sex does not reside only in the genitalia. Our culture's restricted discourse around lovemaking, with its focus on intercourse, is highlighted by one young man's comment eight years after a spinal cord injury in which he lost sensation and movement from the waist down, including the possibility of having an erection… A very inhibitory and largely unexamined assumption in our culture is that sex is penetrative intercourse, and everything else is just foreplay.

Here we see another example of how a client group can provoke debate on normative and religious assumptions around sex – one of the reasons why psychosexual work in religious communities, while challenging, can also prove to be highly rewarding.

Morals and ethics

For the religious therapist, ethical issues may arise and should any of these excluded or forbidden forms of the relationship come to light during therapy. This is because Jews, according to Jewish law, must not support or collude with any transgressions as this would make them accomplices to the transgressions. This can leave the therapist with the challenging task of attempting to reconcile their ethical codes of practice with their personal religious beliefs, which will sometimes be at variance.

Religious and observant therapists walk a difficult road. In belonging to any governing or accrediting body, we are required to subscribe to a professional code of ethics and practice. However, when these codes are at variance with religious laws and rules, it is as though they are being asked to offer therapy with one hand tied behind their back: they cannot, relationally speaking, bring their 'whole selves' into the therapy. That said, it could equally be noted that in facing such dilemmas, they are more able to relate to their clients who are facing similar ethical and moral contradictions and conundrums.

Clearly not all Jewish clients present with the more Orthodox or conventional forms of Judaism. Nevertheless, it is my experience that many clients will carry many ideas and beliefs from the Jewish traditions into therapy. As integrative therapists, not only do we need to be aware of our own feelings when working with this client group, but we also need to be wary regarding which modalities we employ. For example, I believe solution-focused sexual therapy will not work with the more religious or observant Jews because this could simply reinforce traditional views on sex that are limiting and unhelpful. Rather, based on my experience, I believe the most effective approach is to work relationally because this allows for a therapeutic alliance in which the therapist can honour their own beliefs and ethics in a way that can provide the client with alternative perspectives, all in service of supporting the client's desire to change and heal.

The need for this work is growing. A recent research-based report Staetsky and Boyd (2015) looking at the demography of British Jews and Orthodoxy, published by the Institute for Jewish Policy Research, states:

> In particular, we highlight how the Haredi population is growing at an extraordinarily fast rate, due to its rare combination of high fertility and low mortality. By contrast, the non-Haredi Jewish population is declining, not least due to its below replacement level fertility. We note how these measures, combined with an analysis of population momentum over time, help us to develop a probable picture of a future in which the Haredi population will become an increasingly large part of the whole.

This report suggests that there is an urgent need for psychosexual therapist to be prepared for work with those from the Orthodox community.

Conclusion

In the light of the various musings in this work, I would like to present a series of questions that I hope will help psychosexual therapists orientate themselves for work with the Orthodox community.

1. Might couples living within the clearly defined rules and beliefs of Orthodox Judaism feel happy, content and safe within this holding framework – or conversely do we think these constructs are limiting, outdated and lack equality?

2. For those of us who are not Orthodox, are we people who feel difficult accepting and respecting rules, while our clients might not be?

3. Can we see any value in prescribed sexual relationships, for example with periods of sexual abstinence and an emphasis on large families?

4. How might some of the laws relating to Orthodox Judaism be of benefit to non-Jewish couples?

5. What can we extract from the tenets of Judaism that might benefit couples with a different or no faith?

I offer these questions for reflection. Of course, similar questions might be asked of other minority groups with a culture of strict observance to traditional teachings and rulings.

Furthermore, we must not forget the bigger picture in which all our lives exist. It seems clear that religious and cultural persecution is flourishing throughout the world currently. According to Wyatt (2014) there is 'anti-Christian persecution in several parts of the world... Muslims experiencing... a serious degree of persecution and discrimination...

Jewish people in western Europe subject to violence…' This is also a part of our work because this global problem will and does enter the therapy room, impacting on our clients' capacity to be open and free. We must remember, as therapists, that the couple before us is attached to a larger and often troubling environment.

Finally, I would like to conclude with the thoughts of an eminent Orthodox Charedi Rabbi, with whom I originally consulted while preparing this paper. He offered the following insights:

> I think religious attitudes to sexuality may provide a positive framework for the flourishing of meaningfulness of sex, because the notion of sanctified sex can enhance both romance and nostalgia by accentuating the feeling of shared destiny and ultimate oneness as the heart of the pulsating sensuality.

> It is true that it restricts spontaneity, but, when taught correctly, it can fortify the existential meaning of the marital union – as a coming together of two souls rather than just a fleeting material moment. I also think that the Orthodox ethos and the sense of religious duty (obligations versus privileges; responsibility in contrast to autonomy), and the heightened value of marriage and the family unit, encourage people and motivate them to work harder on their issues rather than give in to easier options. But, then again, I am biased!

This book is published with thanks to Rabbi Chaim Rapoport for his support, attention and scrutiny to all aspects of Jewish law.

REFERENCES

Baker, A. (1993). *The Jewish woman in contemporary society: Transitions and traditions.* NYU Press.

Berne, E. (1973). *Sex in human loving.* Penguin Books.

Boteach, S. (1999). *Kosher sex.* Broadway.

Brewer J.S. (1986). *Woman and Jewish law.* New York: Schocken Books.

Fenton, S. (2016, April). Calls for urgent inquiry into sexual abuse of Jewish children in illegal schools. Retrieved from https://www.independent.co.uk/news/uk/home-news/calls-for-urgent-inquiry-into-sexual-abuse-of-jewish-children-in-illegal-schools-a6973571.html

Gaines, J.H. (2018, November). Lilith: Seductress, heroine or murderer? https://www.biblicalarchaeology.org/daily/people-cultures-in-the-bible/people-in-the-bible/lilith/

Hammer, J. (2018, November). Lilith, lady flying in darkness. Retrieved from https://www.myjewishlearning.com/article/lilith-lady-flying-in-darkness/

Goodwach, R. (2005). Fundamentals of theory and practice revisited: Sex therapy: Historical evolution, current practice. Part I. Australian and New Zealand Journal of Family Therapy, 26(3), 155-164.

Heilman, U. (2016, April). Orthodox rabbis wrestle with Jewish law and transgender issues. Retrieved from www.timesofisrael.com/orthodox-rabbis-wrestle-with-jewish-law-and-transgender-issues

Heschel, S. (1990). Jewish Feminism and Women's Identity. In R. J. Siegel & E. Cole (Eds.) Seen but not heard: Jewish women in therapy. New York: Harrington Press.

Katsman, H. (2008, August). Interview with an orthodox sex therapist: Talli Yehuda Rosenbaum. Retrieved from http://www.amotherinisrael.com/interview-with-an-orthodox-sex-therapist-talli-yehuda-rosenbaum

Keshet-Orr, J. (2003). Jewish women and sexuality. Sexual and Relationship Therapy, 18(2), 215-224.

Kleinplatz, P. J. (2010). *New directions in sex therapy: Innovations and alternatives*. Routledge.

Lasson, J. (2000). Improving chatan/kallah education: A piece of c.a.k.e.. Retrieved from https://jewishaction.com/family/marriage/improving-chatankallah-education-piece-c-k-e/

McDonough, K. (2013, April). Israel-based therapist releases sex manual for ultra-orthodox Jews. Retrieved from https://www.alternet.org/israel-based-therapist-releases-sex-manual-ultra-orthodox-jews?akid=10356.4352.-GUXu5&rd=1&src=newsletter828929&t=19

Mishne Torah, Hilkhot Issurei Biah 21:10

Neroulias, N. (2011, May). Study: Orthodox Jews more open to mental health counseling, but needs remain. Retrieved from https://www.huffingtonpost.com/2010/08/14/study-orthodox-jews-more_n_681898.html?guccounter=1

NSPCC (The National Society for the Prevention of Cruelty to Children; November, 2018). Sexual abuse: signs, indicators and effects. Retrieved from https://www.nspcc.org.uk/preventing-abuse/child-abuse-and-neglect/child-sexual-abuse/signs-symptoms-effects/

Maybruch, C., Pirutinsky, S., & Pelcovitz, D. (2014). Religious premarital education and marital quality within the Orthodox Jewish community. Journal of Couple & Relationship Therapy, 13(4), 365-381.

Plaskow, J. (1991). *Standing again at Sinai: Judaism from a feminist perspective.* San Francisco: HarperSanFrancisco.
Reform Judaism.org: https://reformjudaism.org

Rosenbaum, T. (2015, June). Lies my kallah teacher told me: Ten tips for new brides. Retrieved from https://blogs.timesofisrael.com/lies-my-kallah-teacher-told-me-ten-tips-for-new-brides/stated:

Rosenfeld, J. & Ribner, D. (2011). *The newlywed guide to physical intimacy.* Gefen Publishing House.

Kashani-Sabet & Wenger (2015). *Gender in Judaism and Islam.* New York University Press.

Samoylov, M. (2018, November). Orthodox Jews aren't allowed to watch porn. This website helps them cope. Retrieved from https://forward.com/scribe/414512/orthodox-jews-arent-allowed-to-watch-porn-this-website-helps-them-cope/

Siegel R. & Cole E. (1990). *Jewish women in therapy.* New York: Harrington Park Press.

Staetsky, L. D., & Boyd, J. (2015). Strictly orthodox rising: what the demography of British Jews tells us about the future of the community. Institute for Jewish Policy Research.

Weiner, L., & Avery-Clark, C. (2017). *Sensate focus in sex therapy: The illustrated manual.* Routledge.

Weiner, K. (1991). Anti-Semitism in the therapy room. Women & Therapy, 10(4), 119-126.

Weeks, J. (1987). Questions of identity. In P. Caplan (Ed.). The cultural construction of sexuality (pp. 43-63). Routledge.

Wyatt, C. (2014, November). Growing religious persecution 'a threat to everyone'. Retrieved from https://www.bbc.co.uk/news/world-30001063

GLOSSARY

(Definitions primarily taken from www.chabad.org unless otherwise identified)

Baal Teshuvah	Literal translation is 'master of return' commonly understood as a person's state of return to their essential true self.
Ketubah	The ketubah is a binding document which details the husband's obligations to his wife, showing that marriage is more than a physical-spiritual union; it is a legal and moral commitment.
Kippot	The tradition to wear a **kippah** developed as a sign of our recognition that there is Someone "above" us who watches our every action. (Skullcap or *yarmulke*) is a small hat or head covering. In traditional Jewish communities only men wear *kippot* (the plural of kippah) (source: www.myjewishlearning.com)
Madrichim	"Guides," or teacher aides; singular madrich [male] or madrichah [female]. (source: www.templeemanuel.net)
Madrichot	Fem. plural madrichot (as above)
Mechitzah	Separation between the sexes: the partition separating between the men's and women's sections in a synagogue.
Mikveh	Ritual bathing pool in which a person immerses her/himself as part of the transition to ritual purity.
Niddah	Niddah is the period following menstruation, when a Jewish couple separates. After the wife has immersed in the mikvah, they come together again.
Sheva brachot	Sheva Brachot are seven blessings recited over wine during the wedding ceremony, after the wedding feast, and following festive meals during the next seven days.
Tzitzit	Ritual Fringes: (a) Fringed four-cornered garment. (b) The fringes of said garment.

2

IN THE SHADOW OF ABRAHAM

Abraham's Legacy

Introduction

This chapter will introduce the reader to some key aspects of the three monotheist religions of Judaism, Christianity and Islam; I will look at some of their idiosyncrasies, similarities and differences, and offer some thoughts regarding how the teachings of these religions might impact on therapy and how psychosexual and relationship psychotherapists might work with this. While this chapter is written with readers from a Jewish background in mind, I hope the material here will prove beneficial for therapists of any ethnic or religious background working in any aspect of therapy.

To declare my own situation, I am a psychosexual therapist from a white English and nominally Christian background. My interest in this topic has arisen out of my work with clients and an interest in how people of all faiths have absorbed a wide variety of historical teachings, myths and prejudices, whether or not they are conscious of it. And we know that, historically, these prejudices can have terrible consequences – think of the Holocaust; think of the blood libel that has seen Jews accused of murdering Christian babies or poisoning the wells of Christian communities; think of how Islamophobia has demonised the global Muslim population based largely on assumption, hearsay and the rhetoric of right-wing media; equally, I once heard a cultured Jewish woman describing the Holy Communion as a form of cannibalism. Clearly, for both therapists and clients, the ideas that we carry about faith and religion will be a significant factor in the therapy room and will have an impact on our work. For this reason, I want to explore how, as therapists, we might work with religious material in the context of psychosexual therapy. I will begin with a brief overview of the three monotheistic faiths – Judaism, Christianity and Islam – noting various historical and cultural similarities and differences. The content is deliberately selective: I will begin with some general observations, then describe various teachings from the three religions on matters relating to gender, sex, sexuality and relationships. I will include some practical ideas for therapists, and conclude with my belief that the Children of Abraham, like many families, might mutually benefit by becoming closer.

Beginnings

Historically, Judaism is the first of the three monotheistic religions, each of which emerged from the area commonly known in the western world today as the Middle East. Judaism began around 2000 BCE, followed by Christianity two thousand years later, then we have the birth of Islam around 570 CE. These three religions, while differing in belief and practice, share a commonality in that each holds that there is only one God, and that in the beginning God gave his Word (teaching, instruction) to humanity in the form of divine revelation: for Jews the Word came through Moses, for Christians it was Jesus, and for Muslims it was Muhammad.

For Jews, religious law is found in a number of texts, most notably the Torah, which is part of the Tanakh or Hebrew Bible, supplemented by later texts such as the Midrash and the Talmud. The Hebrew Bible is similar to the Christian Old Testament; the Christian New Testament concerns the birth and teachings of Jesus and his disciples. For Muslims, the Qur'an is believed to be the Word of God, directly imparted to Muhammad, arriving as a timeless and eternal message that remains true throughout history regardless of cultural context. Islam accepts parts of the Christian and Jewish texts as divine revelation, notably the five books of Moses, the Psalms of David, and some of the four New Testament Gospels.

The three faiths are connected in having a shared heritage: Judaism and Christianity both hold that their faith emerged through the line of Abraham's son Isaac, while Muslims hold that Muhammad was descended from Abraham's son Ishmael. Hence, all three religions are considered to be people of the Book and Children of Abraham. Indeed, there is a great deal of overlap across the three faiths – such as the traditional belief that God created the world in seven days – but there are also a great many differences. A prime example of divergence is the teaching in Christianity that Jesus is the Son of God, which has led some to question whether Christianity is in fact a monotheistic religion: for Jews and Muslims, God is not a Trinity (i.e. three-in-one: Father, Son and Holy Spirit), nor is there a God on the ground who was resurrected.

Abram – whose name was changed by God to the more familiar Abraham – is the original linchpin that connects the three faiths; he was chosen by God and bound into an eternal covenant. Abraham was an Iron age sheik (Peters, 2004:1) who lived a nomadic life with his extended family until his death in Hebron. After this, Jewish history records the story of Abraham's descendants through the line of Isaac. Solomon succeeded his father King David from whom he inherited the task of building the first temple in Jerusalem, completed in 827BCE. Solomon's reign ended with him displeasing God with his disobedience. After Solomon's death in 796 BCE, the kingdom split into two parts, with ten tribes in the north, which became Israel, and two tribes in the south, led by Solomon's son Reheboam, now known as Judah, which contained Jerusalem and the temple. The Jews resumed idolatrous worship, and rejected God's warnings through his prophets – even stoning Zechariah to death, on Yom Kippur in 661 BCE, when he attempted to prevent an idol being erected in the temple. This eventually led to the invasion of the Kingdom of Israel by the Assyrians circa 740 BCE. The ten tribes were taken into captivity and seemingly nothing more is known of them. This was followed in 587 BCE by the sacking of Jerusalem and the destruction of the temple by the Babylonians, and the execution of thousands of Judeans, while the remaining citizens were led into captivity, except for the poorest who were left to work in the fields and vineyards; this is known as the exile period (Cohen,1986:13; Chabad.org). The theme of the Jewish people's exile and search for their homeland, their oppression and scattering, have recurred until the present day with the establishment of the state of Israel.

Under a less repressive regime led by Cyrus the Great of Persia, who conquered the Babylonians in 539 BCE, the Jews/Judeans were granted permission to return to Judea during the 530s and 520s. After some initial bitter hostilities with the population who had remained, the Jews rebuilt the temple, which was dedicated in 516 BCE. Internally, the next two hundred years saw the end of 'biblical' Israel, with Malachi the last of the prophets. Externally, the Persian period started by Cyrus the Great, in 539, ended with the conquest of Persia by Alexander the Great, circa 333, which inaugurated the Hellenic period. The period of quiescence under their Persian and then Hellenic rulers came to an end in the 160s with the emergence of the Maccabees, formerly country priests, who led an uprising against the Seleucid king of Syria, Antiochus Epiphanes, who had defiled the temple with a statue of Zeus, persecuted Jews and denounced the laws of Judaism. The Hellenic period was a time that saw the canonisation of scripture, the transformation of prophesy into 'apocalyptic', and the writing of various biblical and non-biblical works. Meanwhile, the class of scribes developed and the diaspora continued (Cohen, 1986:15). The Maccabean period, which started in 164 BCE, came to an end in 63 BCE with the successful Roman occupation of Judea, which lasted for six hundred years until 638 CE. However, the unsuccessful rebellion of 70 CE, which led to the destruction of the second temple by the Romans, saw the beginning of a much greater diaspora, with the Jews/Judeans becoming a migratory people with no fixed homeland until 1948.

Jesus

While synonymous with Christianity, Jesus was in fact an observant practising Jew. He was born during a turbulent time. As well as the Roman occupation, there were additional tensions due to an ongoing rivalry between the Jewish sects of the Pharisees and Sadducees. In Jesus, we find a certain common sense and pragmatism, such as his exhortation to render unto Caesar what belongs to Caesar, and unto God what belongs to God: advice that would make sense to millions through the centuries who have had the misfortune of living under occupation. For Christians, it is the New Testament, particularly the Gospels of Matthew, Mark, Luke and John, that teach us about Jesus' dual identity as both Son of Man and Son of God, or Messiah. Among the many New Testament sermons, parables and miracles, the most significant is Jesus' resurrection following his death by crucifixion on the orders of the Roman Prefect; the order was made at the instigation of a group of high priests with whom Jesus had engaged in constant clashes over Jewish law, such as Jesus' denunciation of the moneylenders who worked in the temple – making a profit at the expense of the faithful – which ended with Jesus chasing the moneylenders with a whip: a not so gentle Jesus! Jesus is thought to have lived from 4 BCE until 29 or 30 CE and not much is known about his private life prior to his baptism by John at the start of his ministry, although it appears Jesus never married or had a family. Given his subsequent Messianic status, perhaps the New Testament writers chose to give no more than the barest biographical outlines as part of their wish to emphasise the divine, rather than the human, nature of Jesus.

Muhammad

Muhammad has never been granted Messianic status, always being referred to as Muhammad the Prophet. We know that Muhammad was a family man, however, like Jesus, we are told little about Muhammad's life prior to the start of his ministry. Muhammad (570-632 CE) was born in Mecca, which at the time was little more than a dusty township where nomadic tribes would come to trade under the protection of a sacred truce (Peters, 2004:140). Muhammad was an orphan who reversed his lack of prospects by marrying Khadija, a prosperous older widow, then working for her. At the age of 40, Muhammed started hearing voices. Frightened, he sought advice from a man familiar with Jewish and Christian scriptures who told Muhammad he was receiving the Great Nomas, the Greek name for the Torah. Whatever the truth of this, Peters (2005:14) writes that the Muslim historical tradition had recognised Muhammad as a Prophet in the revelatory tradition of Judaic and Christian prophesy. Through divine revelation, Muhammad received the teachings that have been preserved in the Qur'an. He subsequently preached the Word of the monotheistic God to the tribes in Mecca, though he was not completely successful because the town relied on the trade brought by nomads making pilgrimages to worship at the town's Bedouin pagan shrine.

As with Jesus, Muhammad's preaching and prophesying upset those in charge by threatening the balance of power: both were instances of a prophet not being honoured in their home town. Indeed, after twelve years of preaching, Muhammad faced the threat of assassination. However, fortuitously for him, in Medina, a small impoverished town some 200 miles away, civil war broke out between the two most important Arabic tribes. In 622 CE, Muhammad was invited by the two tribes to arbitrate, which he did, and this led to the establishment of the first home of Islam, which continued to flourish despite the Prophet's death ten years later. Muhammad established a template for Islamic conversion that depended on obedience to his political authority and complete submission to the Qur'an as the Word of God, or Allah as God is known in Arabic.

First centuries of co-existence

Christianity and Islam attracted devout and loyal followers during the lifetime of their respective progenitors, so despite the deaths of Jesus and Muhammad – and, in the case of Jesus, because of his death – these new faiths did not fade away.

Christianity evolved from a messianic Jewish sect into a global religion which, significantly, embraced gentiles as equal with Jews; Christianity became a proselytising religion with a message of life after death that attracted millions. After the death of Jesus, following three turbulent centuries, Rome embraced Christianity and from this centre Christianity spread across Europe and eventually into the Americas and, to a lesser extent, Asia.

Following the death of Muhammad, conquest spread Islam throughout the Middle East and into Asia and across north Africa into southern Europe, leaving behind a visible heritage of beautiful Moorish architecture. In these early years of Islam, Jews and Christians living in the Muslim world were generally tolerated as long as they paid their taxes and recognised their subservient status. This arrangement was formalised in a contract between the three faiths called the dhimma, whereby Jews and Christians who accepted Islamic governance were known as dhimmis (Lewis, 2014:21). Muslims recognised Jews and Christians as being people of the Book and gave them freedom and permission to practice their faiths, though with certain caveats, such as refraining from proselytising, building houses of worship, and making public displays of their religion; neither could they marry a Muslim nor have a Muslim slave. In addition, Christians and Jews had to wear identifying clothing (Peters, 2004:64), which has interesting parallels with both the Nazi command that Jews wear a yellow star and the distinctive clothing of ultra-Orthodox groups like the Haredi.

For a period of around 800 years, from the eighth to the fifteenth centuries, Islam emerged from its dusty tribal roots to become the major religion it is today. During this time there was a largely healthy cross-pollination of ideas between Islam and Judaism, something which is perhaps not widely acknowledged today. Perhaps even more significant is the historical influence on all three religions of Hellenic (Greek) philosophy and ideology. Hellenic beliefs and thought had spread globally, first through the Greek Empire, then through the Roman Empire. What proved most influential was not so much Greek religious practice – the gods of Olympus being not much different from the gods of other polytheistic cultures – but rather the Greek understanding of philosophy, art and science. Indeed, Hellenic philosophy gave a diverse range of cultures a new way of seeing the world that has continued to the present day, influencing Jewish, Christian and Islamic thought along the way.

Jewish law

In western countries today, religious laws play a subservient role to civil and criminal legislation. However, for observant and devout Jews, rabbinical teachings outweigh any national justice system. This is perhaps not surprising given Jews have always tended to live separately from neighbouring or surrounding cultures.

Let's have a closer look at this law. Keshet-Orr (2018:4) offers a succinct description of the two sources of Jewish law:

> Jewish law is derived from two sources. The first is the Scriptures, known as the Torah, which emphasise the Five Books of Moses: this is referred to as Written Law. The second source is the Talmud and Codes, which is referred to as Oral Law. The Talmud is comprised largely of a second-century rabbinic document known as the Mishna, together with the Gemara, which is a commentary

on the Mishna. Because there are many contradictions and tensions within these teachings, rabbinical discourse has been an important ongoing part of Jewish life and tradition since the creation of these various documents.

There are 613 mitzvot, or laws, in the Torah, which are traditionally attributed to Moses, as revealed by God on Mount Sinai. These laws are far-reaching, covering areas such as temple offerings, care for animals, diet, the family, marriage and divorce. There are also instructions regarding behaviour towards non-Jews, which is generally to be kind, although to a select few, such as Moabites and Ammonites, there is an exhortation to war.

The teachings of rabbis are also a central part of Jewish law. Since the diaspora, Jewish courts have traditionally been presided over by rabbis, for whom the study of scripture and the Talmud is their life's work. As an example, the Mishna of Rabbi Judah, a document dating from the end of the second century CE, contains minutely detailed teachings concerning all areas of life. These halakot, or binding legal dictates, are considered to have been derived from scripture or else to have received authorisation "from the tradition of the Fathers", meaning since the time of Abraham.

Christian law

Christian law developed under St Paul from its original Jewish roots to incorporate the teaching of the New Covenant, or New Testament, which Jews and Muslims do not recognise as divine law. As it grew, Christianity established bases in Rome and then Constantinople; the religion gradually gained precedence over the pagan gods of Rome until, in 312 CE, Emperor Constantine was converted and Christianity became the formal religion of Rome. As a result, we can note a key difference between the three religions, namely that, while Judaic and Islamic law were separate from the state, in the case of Christianity, religious law was given equal parity with the well-established civic laws of the Roman Empire. Accordingly, a hierarchy of church leaders, with bishops at the top, held legal as well as religious authority, even being looked upon as descendants of the twelve apostles. In some ways, these first bishops were similar to rabbis in terms of their impact on religious thought, although the subsequent introduction of Christian dogma, which effectively closed down any controversial lines of enquiry, is quite alien to Judaism and rabbinical discussion.

We can observe another interesting difference with Christianity. While the worship of idols is proscribed in all three religions – for example, one of the mitzvot in the Torah reads: "Not to make any figures for ornament, even if they are not worshipped" (Ex. 20:20) (CCN144) – religious statues and pictures are permitted within most strands of Christianity, which is perhaps a result of the influence of pagan Europe on Christianity. Christianity also differs from Judaism and Islam with respect to laws of ritual purity, with Christians today disregarding such rituals and generally being more tolerant of sexual diversity, although, of course, there are still fundamentalist Christians who believe gay people will burn in hell.

Islamic law

Islam holds that sharia – the Muslim way or law – has been revealed by God to Muhammad through the Qur'an. When the Prophet died the pages of the Qur'an were closed, along with the idea that any interpretations of the law were permissible. There is a tradition of hadiths – which are the traditions or customs of the Prophet, as reported by the Companions of the Prophet – however, these hadiths never contradict the teachings of the Qur'an but rather help to explain them. Therefore, in Islam, the Qur'an is scripture, and the tradition of the Prophet and of the Companions could be said to hold an equivalence with the Judaic "time of the Fathers", which was a period of histographical leniency during which it was still an open question whether the revelations of God to the prophets were finished. Subsequently, the holy books have been closed; in the case of the Qur'an, in particular, any interpretation is considered blasphemy.

Islamic law is focused solely on the Qur'an, which traditional Muslims claim as definitive for state law. By contrast, as we have seen, Christianity had the security that came from official endorsement by the state in the form of Rome, while the Jews were essentially stateless citizens so they were in no need of civic laws per se and in their Written and Unwritten laws they had sufficient teachings for their own guidance.

Female gender bias

All three religions are essentially patriarchal, with women's roles clearly defined. Since relatively recently, there have been female rabbis and Christian ministers, but in Islam women may not hold any formal religious status, although Muslim women with a profound knowledge of the Qur'an may serve as family law advisers in the mosque and local community. Traditionally, there has been little inclusion or understanding of feminist thought permitted within the Orthodox Jewish or Muslim communities. The Church of England and other Protestant churches, like the more progressive Jewish synagogues, may have become increasingly liberal, allowing women to be ordained, but neither the Orthodox Jewish community nor the Roman Catholic Church accept women in this role.

In the Roman Catholic Church, the Virgin Mary is sanctified, but neither Judaism nor Islam have an equivalent figure; the idea that Yahweh or Allah could have a mother is an impossibility, a blasphemous thought – and perhaps a similar attitude can be found in Christianity given the doctrines of the Immaculate Conception and the Virgin Birth, both of which ensure that Jesus was not born of an ordinary woman, nor was the Son of God incarnate contaminated by human passion, let alone bodily fluids. Mary, the archetypal Mother, is an important figure for Christian women because she offers understanding and solace in her role as the original suffering mother, while also representing purity/virginity in having a celibate marriage. Indeed, from the perspective of psychosexual therapy, it is interesting to consider that Joseph, the husband of Mary, is widely believed to have been older than his wife: he was a widower, with other children (such as the Apostle James, who was purportedly Jesus' brother) – could it be that Joseph wasn't able to achieve and sustain erections? While, as a Jewish woman, Mary would have known the mitzvot regarding a women's right to sexual consummation ("Not to withhold food, clothing or conjugal rights from a wife"; Ex. 21:10), she was probably not the first woman to forego sexual fulfilment for personal reasons, such as the compensations of affection or financial security.

Within Christianity, we can see that the Jewish law and practice of female ritual purity lost its importance as this new religion spread beyond its Jewish origins and embraced gentiles as followers, including uncircumcised men and women who were ignorant of the law of niddah concerning the pure and impure aspects of the menstrual cycle. It would seem that the concept of purity in Christendom was not concomitant on the ritual laws that concerned sex and the sexual organs, unlike Judaism and Islam. However, virginity was prized in Christianity, with honour killings as much a part of life in areas of early Christendom, particularly in southern Europe's Catholic countries, as it is still a part of life in some Islamic countries.

A disparity across the three religions is their attitude towards divorce. Whereas historically and today Judaism and Islam regard it with a pragmatic tolerance, the church disallowed divorce on the grounds that it was a breach of the holy sacrament of marriage: those whom God has put together let no man put asunder. Henry VIII of England, in the sixteenth century, worked around the prohibition of divorce by succeeding in gaining annulments for his marriages, meaning that in technical terms he was never married. It was not until 1857 that divorce became legal in the

UK, and today the rules of divorce in most western countries have been governed by civil law rather than church law.

Among the three religions, the so-called Christian countries – i.e. countries that are traditionally Christian, although the bulk of the population may not practice the religion – have gained a reputation for sexual impurity, especially since the advent of the pill in the 1960s, which freed western women from the cycle of pregnancy, childbirth and child-rearing with the attendant risks of unwanted children and death in childbirth. However, Christians in Roman Catholic countries in the developing world and in some fundamentalist churches still face a ban on contraception. But for most women in the nominally Christian world, although controversial, the legalisation of this medical innovation proved to be a godsend (with a small 'g'); it more or less freed single women from the fear of pregnancy and the shame of being what used to be called an "unmarried mother" – although the saying that there is no such thing as a free lunch still stands, and no contraceptive method has ever been 100% reliable. The sexual revolution of the 1960s came after two World Wars when, with their husbands serving in the war, women had been called on to run farms and factories, as well as looking after their families, and this led to the emancipation of women, who were given more options than choosing between the roles of Madonna, mother or whore. In this new era women, whose mothers had safeguarded their virginity to increase their chances of marriage, were now free from the yoke of marriage, which had previously been tantamount to being the only financially secure career move open to them. The sexual emancipation of women also caused them to question the teachings of the church, with the traditional church accused of being anti-women due to the restrictions they upheld. At the same time, some attempted to redefine the church's teachings, claiming Jesus was a feminist and in favour of emancipation. This widening rift between the church and society can be seen in the comment of the radical feminist philosopher Mary Daly, who said of the claim that Jesus was a feminist (Heschel, 2015:34): "Fine. Wonderful. But even if he wasn't, I am."

Interestingly, neither male nor female celibacy has a favoured place in Judaism or Islam, where the emphasis is placed on having children and establishing the dynastic line. In traditional Orthodox Jewish households, women – and for this read wives, since being single is not an acceptable norm – face a considerable burden: not only does the onus of keeping a kosher home and raising children fall upon them, but women are often also required to be the breadwinner in order to leave their husbands free to pursue religious studies.

In Orthodox communities, arranged marriages are the norm for young people who, from their late teens onwards, are called on to start a family as soon as possible, often going on to have more children than is the current average in developed countries. Arranged marriages are also typical for traditional Muslim families: parents often select their children's partners, frequently uniting strands of the family for dynastic as well as financial reasons, and several children are the norm. Of course, some Muslims in Britain, parts of Europe and North America are now westernised and possibly allowed more freedom, especially young Muslims who move away from home to attend university or for a job, though daughters are still often expected to return home, even if they went to university. "Marrying in" is still the preferred choice for many Muslims, and virginity, especially in women, is not just prized but a requirement, as it is with Orthodox Jewish communities and observant Christians.

As with their Orthodox Jewish counterparts, traditional Muslim couples are unlikely to have met on more than a few chaperoned occasions before they marry; they will never have been alone as a couple and both partners are unlikely to have had any sexual experience. As a result, sexual difficulties due to a lack of understanding and experience are not uncommon. For men, these difficulties might include over-excitement and rapid ejaculation, difficulty with penetration, difficulty in maintaining an erection, and possibly feelings of guilt, regarding masturbation, which is prohibited in Islam (as it is in Judaism, while often frowned upon in Christianity). For women, difficulties include dyspareunia, anorgasmia and vaginismus, all of which can cause women to dislike or avoid sexual relations. Needless to say, ignorance of sexual and physical functioning can be extremely damaging to a relationship, and such lack of knowledge is common in religious communities in which couples are given little or no instruction and yet are required to switch overnight from the practice of abstinence to a wedded life in which their sexual enjoyment and fulfilment is an expectation.

While there are sexual challenges facing both men and women in all three religions, women have faced the worst of it historically. All three religions have demonised women's sexuality, presenting it as dark and dangerous to men, which is perhaps ironic considering that, until the advent of modern medicine, childbirth has been literally deadly for so many women. Christianity made a cult of lifelong virginal purity while also establishing the corollary of the fallen woman as the inevitable counter-balance; given that few women opt for celibacy an automatic assumption in Christianity is that a woman who enjoys sex might be somehow fallen or "bad", a temptress and a danger to society. Judaism has Lilith, the fore-runner to Eve, a free spirited but reputedly dangerous seductress who strangles babies (Borts, 1994:98-108).

In Judaism and Islam, menstruation has been seen historically as something beyond women's understanding; hence men have taken charge of women's biological and physical functioning, with men applying their superior theological and scholastic knowledge to establish the rules; this is one of many examples where men take the stance of "Don't you worry your pretty little head about it", while reducing the woman and her body to the status of an object. Indeed, in both religions, male dominance and the exclusion of women from scholarly study has always been the norm, especially when it comes to religious texts and traditions. Decisions have always been made for women, not by them, hence heteronormative judgments have come to be seen as inviolate religious truth which cannot be challenged – whereas such teachings can more accurately be regarded as at best misogynist and at worst homosocial (Heschel, 2015:37). Jewish and Islamic scholars have been considered – and have considered themselves to be – experts in different types of menstrual bleeding: for centuries these men have been writing about bleeding that is irregular or overly heavy or long, and about non-menstrual discharge, and so on. There was even a whole book on the subject, the aptly-titled Book of Menstruation, which is attributed to Muhammad ibn al-Hasan al-Shaybani (d.circa 805 CE). Indeed, religious male authority on the subject held dominance until the advent of modern medicine in the late nineteenth century (Katz, 2015:76), when the emphasis shifted to a different type of male authority. In the modern era, men have adopted a sense of clinical detachment on the subject that conjures up Foucault's notion of the medical gaze, which dehumanises and pathologises. This sense of male superiority in all matters, including all matters of sexual functioning and practice, has been incredibly damaging to women physically, emotionally, intellectually and theologically, yet this has been the lot of most Orthodox Jewish and Muslim women throughout history, with some chinks of light in the modern era.

This male insistence on taking control of women's sexuality is probably based in a fear of contamination, which in turn is a fear of death. In modern Judaism, a menstruating woman cannot touch her husband in any way, even to hand him a cup. She must sleep separately during the menstrual period, then observe seven "clean" days before taking the mikveh, or ritual bath, and only then can the physical relationship resume. Should anyone touch a woman during the unclean period, or touch anything she has touched, even accidentally, then they are similarly deemed unclean and commanded to wash themselves and their clothes. During the unclean period, even a handshake between husband and wife is forbidden for fear it may lead to sexual arousal. Islam appears to be rather more relaxed on this subject, encouraging the resumption of intimacy as soon as the woman has finished menstruating: "Once they get clean go to them as Allah commanded you." There is even a confusingly contradictory hadith where the Prophet instructed his wife Aisha, even though she was menstruating, to uncover her thigh so he could rest his head against it and warm himself because "he ached from the cold" (Heschel, 2015:36).

Gender-biased religious teachings also exist for childbirth. In Judaism, according to Leviticus (12.1-8), due to bleeding, the birth of a boy is still followed by seven days of ritual uncleanliness for the mother, while this doubles to fourteen days if the baby is a girl (Jerusalem Perspective, 2019).

A gender bias can also be found in religious teachings concerning divorce. From the sixth to the eleventh centuries – in the Gaonic period (700-1000CE) and in the era of the dhimmi, when Christians and Jews in Muslim areas were permitted to practice their religions with certain restrictions – there was a concern that Jewish women were electing to have their divorce petitions heard in sharia rather than rabbinical courts as the latter were less sympathetic to female plaintiffs. Hence, there was a pressure to modify Judaic law out of a fear that Jewish women might convert to Islam, which would endanger the matrilineal Jewish race (Heschel, 2015: 18). It seems little has changed in Judaism over the centuries: as part of the handover of Palestine in 1948, Orthodox Jewish rabbis were to be given control of the family courts that handled divorce and financial settlements, hence, on the eve of the handover, there was a rush of women wanting divorce suits filed in the British civil court which they assessed would offer a more favourable outcome than they might expect from a rabbinate court. New legislation in 2001 granted civil and sharia courts concurrent rights over everything except marriage and divorce but, due to gender bias and inequality, Jewish, Muslim, Christian and Druze women still rush to file their cases in non-rabbinate courts for a fairer hearing over matters of property, custody and maintenance, etc., while their husbands try to out race them and reach the rabbinical courts first. It is ironic that the same problems and solutions from the Gaonic age still exist in Israel for Jewish (and other) women in the twenty-first century (Joffe, 2015:203-236). The idea of gender inequality and discrimination is perfectly illustrated by the notion that the vagina represents sex and the mouth represents gender (Heschel, 2015:36), which may resonate with many women of various faiths or indeed none.

Circumcision

In Judaism, boys are circumcised at the bris ceremony, which is traditionally held in a synagogue, but sometimes in Jewish homes, taking place on the eighth day after birth, with family and close friends in attendance, the ceremony being carried out by a mohel, a religious man trained to perform the operation. A delay in timing is permitted only if the health of the baby means the ceremony might put him at risk. In Islam, there is no rule that males must be circumcised but there is a general expectation that this will take place. However, in Islam, there is no requirement that the ceremony be carried out by a religious man; in fact, the procedure usually takes place in a clinical setting when the boy is seven years or older and may be performed by a non-Muslim. While circumcision is an inherent part of being a Jewish man, because it was part of the covenant made between God and Abraham, in Islam circumcision is derived from the example of the Prophet, so it is customary, and may be waived for health reasons or in the case of older converts. Christians are not required to be circumcised.

Dietary laws

Islam is less rigorous than Judaism regarding dietary laws – for instance, Islam permits the eating of shellfish. Islam has specific laws regarding animal slaughter although, similar to circumcision, slaughter may be carried out by non-Muslims as long as they are people "of the Book'" and follow Islamic procedure. Dietary laws in Islam allow for dairy and meat to be put on the same plate and eaten with the same utensils, unlike kosher practice where segregation also applies to cooking utensils, pots and pans, washing up, and storage. Judaism permits alcohol and tobacco, both of which are haram or forbidden in Islam. In Christianity there are no dietary restrictions, only conventions such as eschewing meat for fish on Fridays.

Punishment for sexual transgression

Modern Islam has been vilified for the practice of stoning as a punishment for (especially female) sexual transgression. In fact, stoning was originally a Judaic punishment believed to take away the sin of the guilty party (Sonbol, 2015: 50). Accordingly, we can read in the New Testament (John 8:7): "Let him who is without sin cast the first stone." While the point of this statement is that no-one is without sin, the implication is that stoning is inappropriate, which is an example of how Christianity refuted traditional Mosaic law.

Size and security of religions

The three religions differ in size and in the sense of security among followers. Christianity is estimated to have over 2.2 billion followers worldwide, while the global Muslim population is estimated at 2.14 billion; Judaism is much smaller, relatively speaking, with less than 14 million Jews worldwide. In terms of security, Jews have only recently, after centuries of stateless living, found a homeland, and even now this homeland cannot in many ways be deemed a place of total safety. There is no political peace due to the Israel-Palestine situation, and there can be no disputing the fact that the Jews of Israel are significantly outnumbered by Muslim neighbours who bear them ill will. There has also been a global growth in anti-Semitism, with increasing support for Palestine and antipathy towards Israel. Regarding Islam, there has been an increase in Islamophobia in the last twenty years. Within Christianity, there are some countries where Christianity is a minority religion and its followers face persecution.

Religion and psychosexual psychotherapy

It is hoped the foregoing might be useful for therapists. It is likely that our clients may belong to one of the many communities and denominations that exist within these three religions. Within Judaism and Islam in particular, there has been disapproval of therapy, but increasingly this is changing, and it is now common to see private Jewish and Muslim clients or for the NHS and charities to provide counselling and support specifically with Jews and Muslims in mind. Accordingly, it is probably advisable for all therapists to have a basic grasp of religious beliefs and practices, differences and similarities.

There are nuances and differences of belief within each of the religious – so we must be careful not to make assumptions. In Christianity, for example, there are difference between the Roman Catholic Church and Protestant denominations, with the latter including Methodists, Baptists, Jehovah's Witnesses and Seventh Day Adventists. Similarly, the therapist would do well to learn the differences between Sunna, Shia and Wahhabi Islam. At the same time, there are perhaps surprising similarities across the religions and factions: Wahhabi Muslims, for example, could be likened to a dogmatic branch of Christianity or to Orthodox Judaism in that they all adhere to strict laws that are believed to carry an historic authenticity. To give an example, Wahhabi Muslims want to see Islam return to the ideas found in the first three centuries of Sunna, which would see the followers of different types of Islam required to live in particular geographically locations according to where their tradition originated.

Of course, while it is helpful to be familiar with the teachings of different religious and cultural groups, in practice the therapist is extremely unlikely to encounter the adherents of certain groups. For example, a non-Jewish therapist is unlikely to see any Orthodox clients, i.e. clients from a Haredi community, in fact they are unlikely to ever meet a Haredi Jew. Keshet-Orr (2018) offers an excellent overview of the three main Jewish social groups and their historical and geographical background. According to Keshet-Orr, the Jewish people most likely to seek psychological help outside their community are the Liberal, Reform and Conservative communities, while traditional Orthodox Jews would rarely consider seeking help of any form, or even social contact with a non-Orthodox Jew, let alone a gentile. However, there is some evidence that these attitudes might be starting to change, perhaps especially in cases where specialist knowledge may be required, such as with psychosexual therapy, with indications that Orthodox Jews are sometimes willing to seek support outside their community – indeed, it could be said to be an advantage that the therapist does not belong to their tight-knit community because this can allay fears of breaches in confidentiality.

And, in every case, no matter the degree of apparent adherence to religious teachings, there will be under the surface for all clients broader issues of meaning and belief; indeed, there are secret atheists and doubters within every religion.

Same and different – thoughts for therapists

There are some very practical ways in which these various beliefs and worldviews can impact on therapy, and here are some tips for therapists. Conservative and traditional Jewish and Muslim women generally dress modestly, making sure their arms, shoulders and heads are covered, and usually their legs also. Therefore, a female therapist might want to take care that her attire is compatible. Another suggestion is to avoid attempting to shake hands with Jewish or Muslim clients for whom touching is forbidden. Similarly, for couples therapy with strictly observant Jews, the therapist should not encourage the couple to sit close together or hold hands without first checking whether the woman is in her clean period; this point should also be considered when setting any tasks for a couple to do at home, such as sensate focus, which requires touching.

Many clients are uncomfortable talking about sex, but this might be especially difficult and embarrassing for those from a religious and/or ethnic minority background whose culture has not given them opportunities to discuss or learn about sex, let alone gain sexual experience. Sex is likely to have been a taboo subject in the family and community, or perhaps sex was discussed but disguised as conversations about other matters, such as having children or how to keep your partner happy. Accordingly, for such clients, the presenting problem may be a smokescreen: a client talks about their difficulty conceiving, but underneath the client wants the therapist to discern that there are other issues at play and to sensitively make inquiries that will open up these hidden topics.

Therapists will of course vary in their understanding of the different religions – and detailed knowledge is not essential; both having or not having specific knowledge of a client's world can be made use of by the therapist. Therapists with a religious background will have a particular understanding of their communities or, to use a term used in social anthropology, they can take an emic position, meaning their understanding of a social group has been derived subjectively as an insider. Therapists from a different ethnic background to their clients would be holding an etic position, meaning the objective-observer position. Both standpoints can be made use of in the therapy room. However, it is worth remembering that learning the dynamics and social mores of another culture is like acquiring a second language: however fluent you might become, you will never have the felt unconscious understanding of someone who has been submerged in that culture from birth. In Hear Our Voice, a collection of essays by female rabbis, Hadassah Davis (Sheridan, 1994:26-31) describes her experience as a convert to Judaism, offering a frank and moving account of the challenges she faced in struggling to adopt an observant Jewish lifestyle. Davis observes that this lifestyle is something that is easy to assimilate from birth, but hard to acquire as an adult; and, even then, however much the lifestyle is adopted, the convert knows she will never be accepted as being truly Jewish by anyone from an Orthodox or conservative community. Islam and Christianity welcome converts, so Davis's experience is unlikely to be replicated within those religions.

Another distinction in Judaism is the shadow of the Holocaust, which hangs heavily still, with the trauma deeply embedded in the collective unconscious of Judaism, filtering through the post-Shoah generations. The spectre of the Holocaust continues to manifest, resurrected by other life tragedies: consider, for example, how the Holocaust trauma might be retriggered in grieving parents who are desperate to replace their lost child, which is a well-known phenomenon – to fill the empty shtetls, metaphorically speaking, in the hope of securing the future of Judaism. With regards to this phenomenon, Keshet-Orr (2018) suggests that the experience of the Holocaust is the reason behind the recent rise in the birth rate of Orthodox Jews.

Remnants of Israel

It is interesting to consider how a peoples' relationship to God can have an equivalence to marriage and the sexual relationship. The history of Israel's relationship with God, for example, seems to feature relational dynamics that would be familiar to psychosexual and relationship psychotherapists. Indeed, the prophet Hosea likened Israel to his unfaithful wife, whom he forgave and took back as a living example of how God wanted to forgive his chosen people's infidelity to the covenant when they had worshipped false gods. It is also interesting to note in this example that there is an inherent sexism in how unfaithful Israel is cast in the female gender. Indeed, throughout the writings of the prophets, Israel is typically cast in the female role, yet always with an accompanying assurance that she will survive the punishments she must face for her transgressions. The most detailed example of this concept is found in Isaiah 6:13, which describes how the land shall be utterly destroyed and the children of Israel "removed far away", with only a tenth remaining, although even that tenth "shall again be eaten up" – however, a "the holy seed" shall remain (Jewish Virtual Library, 2019). It would seem that fertilising the holy seed is the task that Orthodox Jews have designated as their own, along with upholding the Torah and Talmud in all aspects of daily living.

In 2018, the centenary year of the end of World War I, I heard an audio tape of the last guns to fire in France. As the last breath of gunfire evaporated, along one imagines with any smoke and acrid smell of cordite, the sound of birdsong can suddenly be heard, a sign of life's resurrection. Contrast that sense of hope with the poem Song by Edmond Jabes (1965) which describes the legacy of World War II. Perhaps we can conclude that it is time that all Children of Abraham should begin to focus more on their commonalities than on their differences, and perhaps we might offer our own support in the therapy room.

> At the edge of the road
> There are leaves
> So tired of being leaves
> That they have fallen.
> At the edge of the road
> There are Jews
> So tired of being Jews
> That they have fallen.
> Sweep up the leaves
> Sweep up the Jews.
> Will the same leaves shoot again in the spring?
> Is there a spring for fallen Jews?

REFERENCES

Borts B. in Sheridan, S. ed., (1994). *Hear Our Voice: Women Rabbis Tell Their Stories.* SCM Press, London, UK.

Chabad.org (2019). The Destruction of the First Holy Temple [Online]. [31 January 2019]. Available from https://www.chabad.org/library/article_cdo/aid/144569/jewish/The-First-Temple.htms

Cohen, S.J.D. (1987). *From the Maccabees to the Mishnah.* Westminster Press, Philadelphia, USA.

Davis H. in Sheridan, S. ed., (1994). *Hear Our Voice: Women Rabbis Tell Their Stories.* SCM Press, London, UK.

Heschel, S. (2015). 'Jewish and Muslim Feminist Theologies in Dialogue: Discourses of Difference' in Kashani-Sabet, F. and Wenger B.S. (eds.) *Gender in Judaism and Islam.* New York University Press, USA.

Jabes E. (1965). *Le Retour au Livre* Vol. 111. *Le Livre des Questions,* Gallimand, Paris.

Jerusalem Perspective (2019). Jewish Laws of Ritual Purity in Jesus' Day [Online]. [23 January 2019]. Available from: https://www.jerusalemperspective.com/2646/

Jewish Virtual Library (2019). *Remnant of Israel.* [Online]. [23 January 2019]. Available from: https://www.jewishvirtuallibrary.org/remnant-of-israel

Joffe, L.F. (2015). 'Legislating the Family: Gender. Jewish Law and Rabbinical Courts in Mandate Palestine' in Kashani-Sabet, F. and Wenger B.S. (eds.) *Gender in Judaism and Islam.* New York University Press, USA.

Kashani-Sabet, F. and Wenger, B.S., eds (2015). *Gender in Judaism and Islam*. New York University Press, USA.

Katz, M. (2015). 'Scholarly versus Women's Authority in the Islamic Law of Menstrual Purity' in Kashani-Sabet, F. and Wenger B.S. (eds.) *Gender in Judaism and Islam*. New York University Press, USA.

Keshet-Orr. J. (2018). *Kosher Sex: Psychosexual Therapy with the Orthodox Jewish Community*

Lewis, B. (2014). *The Jews of Islam*. Princeton University Press, USA.

Peters, F.E. (2004). *Children of Abraham*. Princeton University Press, USA.

Sheridan, S. ed., (1994). *Hear Our Voice: Women Rabbis Tell Their Stories*. SCM Press, London, UK.

Sonbol, K. (2015). 'Jewish and Islamic Law: Diffusions of Difference' in Kashani-Sabet, F. and Wenger B.S. (eds.) *Gender in Judaism and Islam*. New York University Press USA

Additional references: not quoted:

Fonrobert, C.E. (2015). 'Gender Duality and Its Subversions in Rabbinic Law' in Kashani-Sabet, F. and Wenger B.S. (eds.) *Gender in Judaism and Islam*. New York University Press, USA.

Lefkavitz, L. (2015). 'Not a Man: Joseph and the Character of Masculinity in Judaism and Islam' in Kashani-Sabet, F. and Wenger B.S. (eds.) *Gender in Judaism and Islam*. New York University Press, USA.

Warrick, C. (2015). 'Dishonourable Passions: Law and Virtue in Muslim Communities' in Kashani-Sabet, F. and Wenger B.S. (eds.) *Gender in Judaism and Islam*. New York University Press, USA.

Printed in Great Britain
by Amazon

75544538R00047